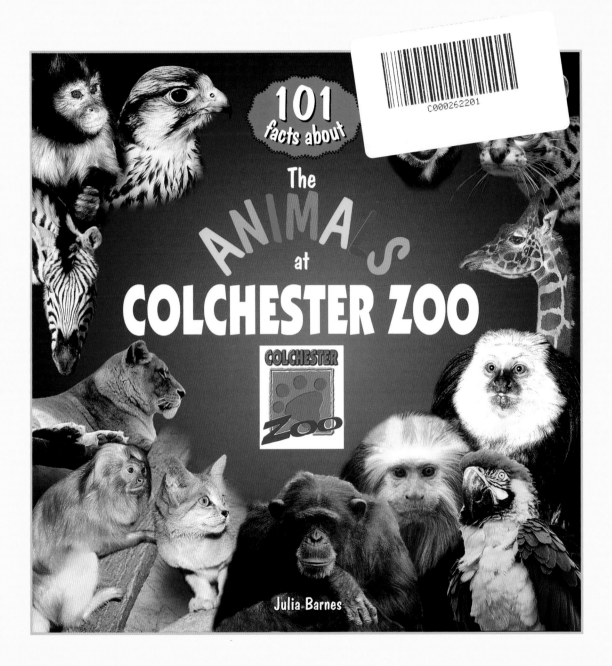

101 facts about

The ANIMALS at
COLCHESTER ZOO

Julia Barnes

First Stone Publishing

Published by First Stone Publishing,
an imprint of Corpus Publishing Limited,
PO Box 8, Lydney, Gloucestershire, GL15 6YD,
United Kingdom.

Design: Sarah Williams

First Published 2005
Text and design © 2005 CORPUS PUBLISHING LIMITED
Photography © 2005 COLCHESTER ZOO

ISBN 1 904439 39 X

Printed in Hong Kong through Printworks Int. Ltd
0 9 8 7 6 5 4 3 2 1

Rhinoceros and Zebra graze side by side, while a Giraffe reaches up for the tastiest leaves. An Ostrich struts past, bending its long neck to find food on the ground. Nearby, there is the sound of trumpeting Elephants, and the roaring of Lions.

Where are you – the Savannah grasslands of Africa? Amazingly, you are in the middle of Colchester Zoo, looking at one of the most spectacular displays of wild animals that has been created by any zoo in the world.

Colchester is home to 200 different species, and in *101 Facts About The Animals At Colchester Zoo* you can find out all about the animals that live at the zoo. You can also learn about the zoo's breeding programmes, which are helping to save animals that are in danger of dying out in the wild.

hunting. A Lioness is more agile than a big, heavy Lion, and she is harder to spot when she is creeping up on her prey.

1 The Lion (above) with his magnificent mane, is the most spectacular-looking animal in Africa, and he rightly deserves to be called the King of the Beasts.

2 But it is the females – the Lionesses (top right) – that do most of the

3 In the wild, Lions are the only big cats that live in family groups. A group, known as a pride, will include around 12 females and their cubs, supported by an adult male.

4 When the Lionesses go out hunting, one will stay behind to guard the cubs. The babysitter will even allow cubs that are not her own to feed on her milk.

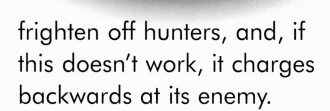

5 It takes a brave Lion to attack an African Crested Porcupine (below).

6 The Porcupine is covered with sharp quills, 30 cm (12 in) in length. It rattles its quills to frighten off hunters, and, if this doesn't work, it charges backwards at its enemy.

7 The Porcupine runs off, leaving its quills embedded in the flesh of its attacker. The quills are almost impossible to remove, and, if the wound becomes infected, the animal may well die.

8 A Zebra (below) provides a tasty meal for a pride of Lions or a pack of Hyenas, and so these animals must always be on the alert for the first sign of danger.

9 Zebras group together on the grass plains of Africa, and, when a hunter sees a mass of striped animals, it becomes confused, trying to pick out a single animal to track down.

10 Different types of Zebra have their own special markings. The Damara Zebra at Colchester Zoo has broad, dark stripes mixed with thin, shadow stripes – but no two Zebras look exactly the same.

11 The Aardvark (above) is the most peculiar-looking animal living on the African grasslands.

12 This is a secretive animal, which emerges at night to sniff out nests of ants and termites. The Aardvark rips the nest open, and scoops out the insects with its sticky tongue.

13 The Warthog (right) has many enemies, including Lions, Leopards, Cheetahs, Hunting Dogs, and even Eagles, and so it has developed ways of defending itself.

14 The Warthog's eyes are positioned high up on its face, so it can see hunters from far away. The Warthog can run surprisingly fast, and, if attacked, its sharp, lower tusks are an effective weapon.

of Spotted Hyenas will chase an animal as big as a Zebra at speeds of 37 miles per hour (60 kph) over a distance of two miles (3 km) before going for the kill.

15 The Spotted Hyena (above and below right) may not look as ferocious as a big cat, but when Hyenas are working in groups, they are among the most effective hunters in Africa.

16 Using a combination of speed and stamina, a pack

17 Nothing is wasted after a kill, and Hyenas will eat every scrap of the carcass – bones included!

18 It is the Vulture that is the true scavenger of the African Savannah.

19 Circling high above the grasslands, Vultures use their incredible eyesight to pinpoint the body of a dead animal.

20 The Turkey Vulture (right) has a sharp, curved beak that is the ideal tool for picking every shred of meat from the bones of a carcass.

21 Like many Vultures, it has no feathers on its head, as they would get matted with blood.

22 The African Elephant (below) is the largest land mammal in the world. Male (bull) Elephants weigh up to 5 tonnes, and females (cows) weigh up to 2.7 tonnes.

23 A cow Elephant is pregnant for 22 months before giving birth to her baby, which is known as a calf.

24 Living on a diet of grass, leaves, and bark, an Elephant has no natural enemies in the wild, and will live for up to 60 years.

25 The White Rhinoceros (above) is one of the greatest survivors of the animal kingdom.

It has been grazing the African grasslands for 40 million years.

26 But now this mighty beast is in danger of dying out. Rhinoceros horn is highly valued in Chinese medicine, and, as a result of hunting, numbers in the wild are falling fast.

27 There are no prizes for guessing that the Giraffe (right) is the tallest animal on earth. A male can reach a height of 5.3 m (17 ft), and a female will be around 4.5 m (14.5 ft) tall.

28 The Giraffe reaches up to the top branches, and uses its tongue, which is 30 cm (12 in) long, to pull off leaves. The tongue is blue-black in colour so that it does not get burnt in the scorching African sun.

29 The Ostrich (below) is the tallest bird in the world, measuring up to 2.75 metres (9 ft). It cannot fly, but it can run as fast as the wind, reaching speeds of 60 kmh (37 mph).

30 The Bateleur Eagle (above) spends most of the day on the wing. It glides over the African grassland and may cover up to 200 miles in a single day. The name Bateleur comes from the french word for acrobat, as this eagle specialises in performing spectacular somersaults in the air.

31 The colourful Mandrill (below) lives in the rainforests of west Africa, foraging for fruit, insects, and seeds.

32 These exotic monkeys face two great threats – they are hunted for meat and their home is being destroyed.

33 Colchester has a breeding group of Mandrills, which is the largest in the UK.

34 Colchester is the only zoo in England where you can see the rare Gelada Baboon (above).

35 Gelada Baboons come from the mountainous regions in Ethiopia. They have got so used to living on the ground that they cannot climb trees.

36 The male can inflate the red skin on his throat and on his chest, so that he looks really menacing.

37 The Chimpanzee (left) from western Africa is one of our closest living relatives in the animal kingdom.

38 Chimps are so intelligent that they have learnt to use tools. For example, a Chimpanzee will use a stick to fish out termites from a nest.

39 Deserts are the world's driest regions, and only a few animals can survive in the harsh conditions.

40 In Africa's Sahara Desert it is boiling hot during the day. The Fennec Fox (right) has huge ears that act as a cooling device, as well

as allowing it to hear animals moving over the sand.

41 The Sand Cat (left) comes out at night to hunt for rodents, small reptiles and birds. It has fantastic night vision – six times better than ours.

superb hunter. Flying high over the Sahara Desert, it will launch a surprise attack to catch a bird in mid-air.

44 Moving at speed, the Lanner Falcon will drop down on its victim, and will hit it so hard that the sound can be heard some distance away.

42 The Sand Cat has long hairs covering the bottom of its paws, which stop it sinking in the sand and protect its pads from the heat.

43 The Lanner Falcon (above) is a

45 If birds are in short supply, the Lanner Falcon will swoop to the ground to pick up a lizard.

46 At Colchester Zoo, you can see how different animals have adapted to life in the steamy, hot, tropical rainforests of South America.

47 Brilliantly coloured Macaws (right) live in the rainforest canopy, where the tall, straight trees branch out and sunlight filters through the leaves.

48 The Macaw is one of the noisiest birds in the rainforest. It has a sharp, curved bill that is ideal for cracking nuts.

49 Spider Monkeys are the acrobats of the forest, swinging from tree to tree, with ease.

50 The Spider Monkey (right) can hang on to a branch just by its tail.

51 The Buffy-headed Capuchin (below) lives in the understorey of the rainforest, where trees grow closer together and the light is dimmer.

52 Capuchins are good climbers, but they also descend to the forest floor to look for food.

53 The destruction of rainforests means that animals, such as the Buffy-headed Capuchin, are in danger of dying out.

54 Marmosets and Tamarins are small, squirrel-like monkeys that live in the South American rainforest. Many species are now under threat in the wild.

55 As well as facing the danger of losing their forest home, these beautiful, silky-haired monkeys have been trapped for the pet trade.

56 The Golden Lion Tamarin (right) generally gives birth to twins. This is true of all

Tamarins and Marmosets and sets them apart from other monkeys.

57 The male Golden Lion Tamarin takes an active part in rearing the young, helped by older offspring in the family group.

Lion Tamarins left in the wild, but now zoos like Colchester are actively involved in breeding programmes.

58 There were fewer than 300 Golden

59 Geoffroy's Marmoset (left) lives in family groups of 8-10 animals, consisting of a male and a female, and their offspring.

60 They move through the trees, looking for fruit and insects. They also have specially adapted teeth so that they can feed on tree sap.

61 There is a huge variety of reptiles and insects living among the trees and on the forest floor.

62 The Green Iguana (right) can grow up to 2 m (6.5 ft) in length, but it is agile enough to climb among the trees of the forest canopy, which may be 30 m (98 ft) above ground.

63 Living off a diet of fruit, insects, and sometimes small mammals, the Green Iguana can also be found in swampland.

64 The Green Iguana is a good swimmer, and, if it is in danger, it will drop from an overhanging branch into a pool and swim to safety.

65 The Blue Poison Dart Frog (below) secretes a poison from its skin, which is deadly to many animals.

66 This frog makes its poison by eating a certain type of ant, which contains toxic chemicals.

67 You can see Leaf-cutter Ants (above) in a procession, carrying tiny segments of leaves to their nest.

68 The leaves are used to feed a fungus, which the Ants grow in an underground chamber. The fungus provides food for the Ant colony.

69 The Margay (right) is a small cat who lives in the canopy of the South American rain forest. It is a brilliant climber, and can scamper headfirst down trees.

70 It is rare to see the Margay, who sleeps during the day and hunts at night in the thickest parts of the forest.

71 The agile Margay catches birds and small monkeys , as well as searching for tree frogs and insects.

72 We think of penguins as living in cold regions, but Humboldt's penguins (right) live in the warm waters off the rocky coast of Peru and Chile.

73 Penguins, which are classed as birds, look clumsy on land, but in the waters they swim effortlessly at speeds of up to 32 kph (20 mph).

74 The Patagonian Sealion (left) is strong and fast in the water, and will hunt penguins as well as catching fish and squid.

75 The male Patagonian Sealion is nearly three times as big as the female, weighing up to 340 kg (748 lb).

24

76 On the other side of the world, Asia has its own tropical rainforests. Some species of animals are similar to South American rainforest dwellers, but at Colchester Zoo you will see some animals that are unique to Asia.

77 The Binturong (right) looks like a cross between a bear and a cat. It lives among the trees, gripping on to the branches with its sharp claws and its strong tail.

78 The Binturong is only active at night, and can see well in the dark. It also relies on its hearing, and its sense of smell, when it is hunting for birds and small mammals.

79 The Orang Utan (below) is so well adapted to living in the trees that it rarely goes down to the forest floor. It has long arms to swing through the trees, and both its hands and its feet are hooked so that it can grip the branches.

80 The Orang Utan does not have many muscles in its face, and so it cannot pull different expressions. It relies on sound to communicate with other animals.

81 A loner by nature, the Orang Utan is in danger of dying out in the wild, as its home is being destroyed.

82 The Lar Gibbon (right) starts the day with a 15-minute 'song' to proclaim its territory and to cement bonds in the family group.

83 Then the Lar Gibbon travels throughout its territory looking for fruit to eat. It swings from tree to tree, and can leap a distance of 15 m (49 ft).

84 Finding a comfortable place to stop and eat is no problem – the Lar Gibbon has an extra-thick pad of skin on its buttocks so that it can squat in the branches.

87 Threatened by the destruction of its home, hunted for its meat and skin, the Macaque faces danger on many fronts.

88 The Lesser Malayan Chevrotain (top right) forages on the forest floor looking for fallen fruit, leaves and grasses to eat.

85 The Lion-tailed Macaque (above) lives in small troops in the upper storey of the rainforest.

89 These shy animals have many enemies, including Leopards, Pythons, Eagles and Crocodiles, so they only venture out at night to feed.

86 Females cannot breed until they are five years old, and will only breed twice in their life.

90 The Asian Short-clawed Otter (below) is as much at home in water as on land. Its long, streamlined body is perfectly adapted for swimming.

91 When an otter dives underwater, it closes its ears and nostrils and uses its whiskers to find frogs, fish and crabs, which it catches with outstretched hands.

92 Asian Short-clawed Otters are sociable animals and they have 12 different calls to communicate with each other.

94 Active at dawn and at dusk, the Red Panda is a slow-moving animal that spends more than half the day asleep.

95 Bamboo shoots are its favourite food, but the Red Panda will sometimes climb down to the ground in search of grass, roots and insects.

93 In the Himalayan forests, the climate is much cooler than in a tropical rainforest. This is the home of the Red Panda (above) – although it is now very rare in the wild.

96 The Bengal Tiger, from India, has an orange body with black stripes, but occasionally a white cub is born.

97 In the wild, a white Tiger (above) stands little chance of survival because it is so easy to spot. There are only 100 white Tigers alive today, living in zoos.

98 In the wild, all Tigers are in danger. Their homes are being destroyed, and they are hunted for their fur and for their whiskers, which are used in Chinese medicine.

99 The Amur Tiger (below) roams the forests of Russia and China. It is the biggest of the five species of tiger – an adult male may weigh as much as 318 kg (700 lb).

100 A top-class hunter, the tiger creeps up on its prey and then uses an explosive burst of speed to get close enough to pounce.

101 There are only 400 Amur Tigers left in wild. Colchester Zoo has one female Amur tiger and is hoping that she will soon be joined by a male to start a breeding programe. It is vital that we support Colchester – and other zoos – in the battle to save the tiger, and many other of the world's most amazing animals.